talking in the dark

GO THERE.

OTHER TITLES AVAILABLE FROM PUSH

Cut
PATRICIA McCORMICK

Fighting Ruben Wolfe
MARKUS ZUSAK

Kerosene
CHRIS WOODING

Crashing
CHRIS WOODING

Pure Sunshine
BRIAN JAMES

Tomorrow, Maybe
BRIAN JAMES

Nowhere Fast
KEVIN WALTMAN

I Will Survive
KRISTEN KEMP

You Remind Me of You
EIREANN CORRIGAN

You Are Here, This Is Now:
The Best Young Writers and Artists in America
EDITED BY DAVID LEVITHAN

Martyn Pig
KEVIN BROOKS

Born Confused
TANUJA DESAI HIDIER

talking in the dark

a poetry memoir

by Billy Merrell

SCHOLASTIC INC.

**NEW YORK   TORONTO   LONDON   AUCKLAND   SYDNEY
MEXICO CITY   NEW DELHI   HONG KONG   BUENOS AIRES**

No part of this publication may be reproduced in whole or in part, or stored in a retrieval system, or transmitted in any form or by any means, electronic, mechanical, photocopying, recording, or otherwise, without written permission of the publisher. For information regarding permission, write to Scholastic Inc., Attention: Permissions Department, 557 Broadway, New York, NY 10012.

ISBN 0-439-49036-7

Copyright © 2003 by Billy Merrell. All rights reserved. Published by PUSH, an imprint of Scholastic Inc. SCHOLASTIC and associated logos are trademarks and/or registered trademarks of Scholastic Inc.

12 11 10 9 8 7 6 5 4 3 2   7 8/0

Printed in the U.S.A.   40
First Scholastic / PUSH printing, October 2003

Contents

1. to my dad, parents, family

Runaway	3
Folding Sheets	5
Photo-booth Narration	6
Hide-and-Seek	7
Hole	8
Letter to Our Parents	10
Back at the Playhouse	12
Lessons	13
When It Was Still Their House	15
Mother	16
Waking the Family	17
Player Piano	18
Lures	19
Memorial	21
Heaven	23
To My Dad, Parents, Family	24
Every Year	25
Orphan	26
Aubade to Childhood	28

2. giving it wings

Sleepover	35
Give It Wings	36
Talking in the Dark	37
Cologne	38
This Bird Has Flown	39
Following	43
Cover	46
Canon	47

Smoking 48
Histories 49
Before 51
A Subtle Shade of Blue 52
Look at Me 53
On Remembering What I Wrote to You 55
Teeth 56
Only Pretending 58
Yes 60
3½ Love Sonnets 62

3. to the living

To the Living 67
What I Hope Dying Is Like 68
Still 69
The World, and More 70
What the Body Allows 72
A Dream for a Boy 73
Prayer for a Son 74
Shaving Poem 75
My Father, Reading to Me 77
Back to Life 78
A Later Innocence 79
Pietà 81
Gift 83
She Predicted You 84
Sudden Arrangement 85

4. work

October 89
Confession 90
Sketch 91

Secrecy   92
A World, in Two Parts   94
From Breaking   96
Because   97
Work   98
Soundtrack   100
Boxes   105
December   106
Your Opening   107
Apologia   108
Anatomy   110

5. coming into adagio

Looking Back   115
Ginger   117
The World, Without Us   118
That Moment, Remembering   121
Portraits   122
Shhh   124
Tattoo   125
Intimacy   126
The Promise   127
Answer   128
Breakfast   129
Still Life   131
Welcoming   133
Moth   135

For my parents
Cathy and David Lloyd, and Duane and Carol Merrell
for showing me love in the beginning
and for teaching me to build a life with it.

Acknowledgments

I would like to thank the instructors who have given me so much of themselves: William Logan, Michael Hofmann, Brandon Kershner, Julisa Delamar, Holly Leake, and Jacqueline Jones. I would also like to thank my friends and family who have carried and sustained me, especially Brian Merrell, Carl Holder, Edward Spade, Nico Medina, Michael Renehan, Laura Heston, Misty McIntyre, Natalia Jacovkis, and Alice Wallace—you have given me more than you know and I am most grateful. Further thanks to Jean Feiwel and Craig Walker for their support of the PUSH internship, as well as Anica Rissi and Eireann Corrigan for their involvement. Most of all, I would like to thank my friend and editor David Levithan for much more than I have space for here—without your generosity this book would not have been written, and without your presence my life would not be nearly as charmed. Literogratumerriment!

1. to my dad, parents, family

Runaway

If we are in trouble or bored enough
Brian and I run away. Reckless,

we imagine, with our parents' love, or cautious,
even, with our own — we know we'll return

and, probably, so do they. We sneak around
to the back of the house and watch them search

from room to room before we come back
to knock on the door like salesmen.

When they answer we are strangers. My brother
introduces himself as Jake and I, given the chance

to name myself, am Leaf. My father plays along,
offers us dinner, and explains that his children

have run away. He says he is in search
of some new ones — us, if we behave. So I eat

all of my mashed potatoes and show my mom
the clean plate and my brother smiles as often

as possible. They ask him where we are from
and why we left and I giggle as he answers.

We must seem like charming new kids, except
I can't handle my new identity, screaming

my new name whenever I see a plant. All that
seems to change is how the scene plays out.

Sometimes, we forget all about our game, and others
I annoy my dad until he sends us away.

Usually though, our parents pretend to cry
in the kitchen until our hearts break and we set out

into the yard to find their children, and return
as Brian and Billy. We help in the kitchen, apologize

for making them worry, and they forgive us
until I giggle, giving us all away.

Folding Sheets

It was just the two of us then, a sea of linen
between us, her at one end, me at the other.

And then she said *lift* and the sheet went up
like a white whale, or a hill rising up to be born

out of the earth, a wave slowly swelling, beginning
to break. And then the air underneath is undone

like hands just after a prayer. Just before
the sheet went slack, she said *okay* and I would

run to her, to hug her, to press my face into the fabric
of her belly. Held there by the moment memory makes

huge and soft, I fell into my mother as I would to Earth.
She'd say to hand over my corners. Let go, reach down,

back away, lift again. Our sea grew heavy from being folded
and folded. Nothing was like that first white rise and fall,

that first huge ballooning and breathing out,
all space ours and so little between us, then.

Photo-booth Narration

There is a strip of pictures
I found in a box and kept
in secret. Four frames: my father
all hair and tint and huge grin.
And then another, my mother
leaning in for a kiss, the booth

filled for the moment by the sheer
youth of their love. And then
she is gone, my father left
laughing. It is the seventies,
years before I will be born.
These are the parents I will

never know: my father's
full head of hair, my mother's
stolen affection. This is
the love I was too young to
witness. I knew it was there,
even in that old house, after

I was born. It was there,
even then — not quite
filling it, but filling
envelopes and albums,
cabinets and boxes.
My brother and me.

Hide-and-Seek

Like any second son, I learn to play alone.
My mom tries to teach me her lonely games:
solitaire, cross-stitching, counting backwards

from a million. I don't understand the customs
of solitude and am one-half of any game, in practice
for my brother. I play hide-and-seek by myself,

hide under the sink or behind the comforter
in the linen closet. I sit in the dark and wait
for someone to come and find me. Dangerous

charades: I pretend to wait for my seeker
as silently and as long as possible. It is dark
in the closet and darkening outside, only a thread

of light at the foot of the door. It's nearing
time to emerge when I hear my mom answer
the phone. She paces, paces, then sits

on the couch so close to the door
I can hear her quiet sobbing and wonder
if she can hear me breathing. Even then, I know

if I open the door I'll scare her. So
I hold my breath and start my counting.
It seems like years before I open the door.

Hole

The first house I remember
being mine was big enough
for our small family. A small time

after Mom moved out, Dad left
the doors unlocked and the weeds
grew and grew until our neighbors

complained, then finally built a fence
to keep us away. My brother and I
took over the street and our friends

joined us to play Savage and drink
straight from the hose. When a ball
rolled into the sewer, we called

for our fathers to come together
and lift the grate. And I was
lowered like a casket into the dark.

In high school, my favorite story
was "Hole," about a boy whose friend
died after climbing down into a sewer

to get something. He too went down
but decided he liked the dark. If I had
read it then I wouldn't have

insisted we go after the ball. I would have
shrugged the game over, a coward,
and gone home, where I'd feel

closed off, some unknown
calm disturbed. Closing and locking
the doors, I'd have let it fall away

and be gone.

Letter to Our Parents

For whatever reason, I've always thought you understood
more than me. I was seven, and remember you
loving each other, then not. Scenes remembered through

home videos: my birthday, I open the closet and find a bike,
fast forward to the two of you kissing in a doorway, pause
just before you dodge the lens, rewind to Christmas,

pause the kiss that ends too quickly, watch you exchange gifts.
I could go on like this; I love to remember when we were
together — not because I want it back, but because it is

a part of us. Maybe if I had been older, maybe if I remembered
crying instead of just waving goodbye as Mom pulled out
of the driveway, maybe if I remembered Dad

telling us Mom wouldn't come back, I would be able
to cry for the four of us then. I wasn't old enough
to know how things were meant

to work. At the apartment Mom rented before
moving in with David, Brian and I chased ducks and raced
among stucco buildings. I've always thought you understood

more than Brian and me. But now I know you were too busy
falling out of love to know what was going on. Brian and I
found a stream one day while trying to get lost.

He made me drink the rest of my Coke, wrote something
on a receipt, put it in the bottle, let it float away.
I want to go back and ask him who he hoped would find it.

Rewind to just before he threw it in, pause and see
if I can make it out. Read that letter he wrote to you both.
Close in enough to read him — I want to know how badly he
   took it.

Back at the Playhouse

I am six or seven when Christy says
to come with her into her playhouse.
I don't see why not and have always
wondered what it looks like inside.

She undoes her pants and says to
undo mine. She is seven or eight,
but one year older than me and four
inches taller, so I do. There we are,

two kids, curious, nervous, naked
from the waist down, when her father
opens that little pink door and
finds his daughter in my arms.

All I remember is running home,
crying but being afraid to tell my dad
because I've done a bad thing. Not sure
why or what, but something.

Lessons

I'm not sure why, but Dad has sat us down,
Brian and me, and we are being taught how to eat

properly. I don't know where my elbows should go
if not on the table, and can't imagine chewing without my mouth

allowed to open. My father listens and we are to chew
as quietly as possible so Carol will like us. When we go

to her house for dinner, we drink only milk and her children
eat half of their food while my brother and I finish

what's on our plates and then more, with a hunger that seems
endless, and manners that I am afraid seem new or, worse,

unfinished. Carol is pretty in an unsuspecting way I'm not
used to. And I watch her, because we are taught as boys

to watch the girls that are pretty. I want her to like me,
but she has to remind us to wash our hands

and I'm scared I am going to mess something up.
One Sunday, Carol and her kids are going to church

and I come along, learn to make chicks out of yarn and paper,
get my own Bible. It already has my name on it, gilt

and gleaming off the cover, though I never asked for it. The pages
are gold-edged too and there are pictures inside of stories

I have promised to learn: Moses, Noah, Jesus seated with children
as if posed in a Sears portrait. I'm going to like it, this new, clean me.

But I can't help but feel out of place. I have borrowed her son's shirt, since Carol didn't think any of mine were appropriate, so I feel

posed too, rehearsed, transparent, the new boy in a good world that is welcoming but was full enough without him.

When It Was Still Their House

Brian slept in their living room and I was learning,
in the sixth grade, about segregation. The way we divide
ourselves cleanly apart. I slept in the addition

to the old house — it was the only room with carpet.
I could pull it up where it was loose and hide
little things that were flat and worth being found:

Elvis stamps I was sure would be worth something
someday, a card from my grandmother, Kool-Aid points.
But the things most worth hiding aren't flat

so I buried a metal box behind the garage under generations
of pine needles — not deep, not into the soil, but covered.
Lea and I played in the azaleas while Bob and Brian stalked

in that margin where my box was buried, where they peed
in secret and were scolded when found out. My stepbrother
and I were the same age, so I didn't understand why he was okay,

old enough for Brian if I wasn't. One morning,
when I woke up and one of the six of us was in the shower,
I didn't know if I could hold it in, so I snuck outside to go, afraid

someone would know, afraid to be seen and made fun of
while my little box hid, empty but wanting so badly to be
filled. As badly as I wanted to have something to hide.

Mother

Lea still has her doll collection, so I still have my favorite:
the small one with the eyes that close

when you put her down. It's the one she gave me
to baby-sit with her when Brian and Bob wouldn't

have me or I didn't want to play by their rules.
I remember asking Lea if the doll was mine and she said No,

because, of course, she was Lea's and should never belong
to a boy. Lullaby so quiet not even the baby can hear.

At first I don't know why she's crying. But I have to
calm her. The way only a mother can calm her child —

because she knows where on the back the hand presses,
if and when to lift and for how long. But I am a boy,

her boy, and am not strong enough to lift her, though
I love her and would love to.

Waking the Family

I used to love waking first. In the house, awake,
I would go into the kitchen, my feet the first
to warm the tiles. Room to room, I'd find the
evidence of time's settling: the dishwater

flat, the froth broken, the fan no longer on and the stove
finally cold. One by one I'd turn things back on.
Stir the dust, make some toast. Wake the house
without waking the family.

I used to love waking. First in the house awake,
I would get into the bath, feet first. Lower myself
slowly under, line of the water's surface up
to my shoulders then neck then ears. And by the time

my whole head was under, I could hear the water
quiet in the plumbing. No one awake but me,
nothing running, no one else to rattle the pipes. I would
hold my breath as long as I could, imagining

a world as still as water, pretending I was
lonely, without actually being alone.

Player Piano

Alex died with a mouthful of cedar
and I buried him behind the garage and cried
while the three of them laughed

at the expression on his face, how
even his hair seemed stiff and dead,
how he hugged at the cage floor,

not wanting to go. Your father dies,
and I think of the bald corduroy of his
Sunday suits, the sweet pastel of mints

he excavates from the depths of his pockets.
Goodnight. His closed lips seem to say
there is no point in being afraid of death.

You pull the sheet up over my shoulders
and kiss my forehead. *Goodnight.* That night
I am only a body.

       I spend a night at a friend's house
and hear for hours, from down the hallway,
what I'm sure is a piano — the infinitesimal

yet endless percussions play themselves to sleep.
I never question who the litany is for, instead
imagine your father's piano, how he taught me

to load and reload those yellowed scrolls.
My legs aren't long enough to pedal with my feet,
so I climb down, sit under that great box

and knead the relentless metal into motion.
The constellations unwind.

Lures

I don't know where my mother was, but I have
a picture David took of me. I am so small,
young — I must be nine or ten — and tiny

in the frame, half an inch among the half-lit yard.
Orange and pink now, the photo itself is a picture
of time, evidence of age and where we were then.

In David's yard on Cesery, he tried to teach me
corkball and how to gut a fish. And I thought loving
my mother, to him, was loving me, something forced

for the sake of their new marriage. So I let him teach me
to mow the grass in concentric squares, each fitting
into the one before, the unkempt made smaller

and smaller with each lap. When David's friends
were over and I was in the way, David called me a fairy
and I wouldn't stop crying until Mom pulled me into a room

and explained the workings of his love, how that was his way
of showing it. I didn't believe her, but she promised,
saying he didn't know how to be a father

to boys who made A's and painted pictures,
who didn't play sports. I helped Mom in the kitchen
and Brian played video games, while David

spent the whole day in the little room
where he kept his lures. Mom would say to get him
for dinner and I would knock at the door, smiling

because I always smiled then. In the picture, I am
looking forward to him and waiting for him to say cheese.
But he just shoots away. So I am left waiting

for a wave, any gesture of closure, anything
to prove he is keeping my mother's promise.

Memorial

I am in my room or reading
on the couch when David comes in
and asks me to come outside.
There is a familiar quality
in his voice, strange insistence —
I've heard it a few times before
when he's asked me to hurry
into the living room. I think
something's wrong, but it isn't.
He just wants me to see a girl
on TV that he thinks is hot
or there is a documentary on
WWII or Vietnam and he wants
to share that fear with me.

But this time he is calling for me
to come outside. It is summer
and he probably needs a hand
hauling something from the garage
or handling something in the yard.
How long is this going to take?
But he just wants me to stand by him
as he looks up at the flag he puts up
every year. I don't know it is
Memorial Day, only that it is Monday
and I'm not in school.

And then he starts talking
and I still don't know why
until he mentions the war.
I think he is going to
look at me, or put his hand
on my shoulder, but he's not
my father so he just starts

remembering Vietnam like
a bullet remembers its impact.
He doesn't say that, exactly —
he doesn't know how to say that.
Though I think I know
what he means until
he says how green it all was.

What? I think of *Platoon*
or *Good Morning, Vietnam*
and the color of wet money.
*It was so green. It rained green
and we wore green — everything.
But when we put up that flag . . .*
So I imagine seeing color
for the first time — and when
I open my eyes he is looking
at me. But he is finished, so I
go inside, where I don't know
what to say, so don't.

Heaven

David took us to Kingsley Lake, to that place
he went for his senior trip. I pass it now
on the road from Jacksonville to my college town.
It is a cheap place to swim — which is perhaps why
we went that Saturday, when it was ninety-something
degrees and the window unit couldn't cool that
old house. I imagine him, somehow no younger,
poor boy on a bus, barely able to graduate, and later,
climbing up that tall wet ladder toward the sky.

He is my stepfather, but it seems inadequate
not to call him father too when he has spent
thirteen years silently trying to be. He took his daughter,
my brother, and me, and the three of us climbed
that same ladder, knowing at the top we would look down
and be afraid to jump. He waited in the water at the bottom,
laughing, as Kelli and Brian looked over the edge.
But I didn't look, only leaped forward, held
by four seconds of air, that hungry, dry ether.

Is that what Heaven is like — four seconds
and a splash? You spend your whole life afraid
of stepping out of the body that has become
all you know. And when you do step out,
or leap from that windy edge into all of that
brightening light, maybe you'll wish
you could go back and die over and over.
I know I closed my eyes that whole way down,
so it makes no sense that I can now remember
David's face when I jumped for the first time.

To My Dad, Parents, Family

I have a hard time writing poems
that blame you. Not that I try to, but

it occurred to me to tell it how it was
and it sounded so much like

I was complaining. So I stopped
because it didn't matter then

so why should it now, because
we can't change anything and,

most of all, because I love you
and it hurts to think you'd take it

any other way.

Every Year

Christmas eve, my mother puts on "O, Holy Night," plays it
over and over. At first she is singing along, moved to crescendo,

but soon she is smoking on the couch, then walking to turn it off,
quickly, because she is suddenly brought to tears. Kneeling

on the blue carpet, head in hands. I am to hold her, rock my mother,
roles reversed suddenly because she has fallen, as if from her bike or

out of love, but further. And though I know she can feel my chest
against her heaving back, and though I know she can hear me

saying *it's okay, it's okay* — against Reba's voice, singing
unyieldingly as if from somewhere separate from this world.

My mother is all breath and tears, all heart against back.
I wonder if she knows I am there at all, and then

she grasps my arm: reaching for a railing in the dark. I say *I love you*
and she begins but I hold her more tightly, *I know, shhh.* I know

this isn't about me. This is about her father, who has died. For her,
this is about a love that follows the dead but which does not itself
   die.

And for me this is less about him, that man who was gone
before I learned how to remember, than about the future. It's like

the moment I first saw my father taking his blood pressure. I am
my mother's son and one day, I'm learning, they too will die.

Orphan

When my grandmother dies, just after Christmas,
my mother, stunned as a child, sudden orphan, flies us up
to Michigan for the funeral. David, born and raised in Florida,

is as excited to see the snow as Brian and me. At the reception,
he watches the window from my mother's side. We don't know
what to say, any of us. I loved her my whole life, a thousand

miles away. And though I remember climbing up
into her lap to be held, there is nothing close
to a tear in my eye — and why should there be?

To me, she is no more gone and no less
with us. Before the funeral, my uncle Steve
reads his children books explaining death. Hugely

Catholic and the warmest of fathers, he sits before them,
trying to explain loss in terms of their faith. Sixteen,
I'm not sure I can even understand. When we are

finally in the church, all of us who loved and love her
sit together before the urn which, my mother explains,
does not yet contain her mother's ashes. So I think,

why now, why here? Too young to understand
the need to let go, no reason yet — or need —
to believe in heaven. But as the priest begins

I can feel myself leaving my body. I am outside,
somewhere, in the snow. Slow cataracts of white
burying me. Until he says the verse that always

made my mother cry — carved in wood by her father
and hung in her bedroom — *now these three remain: faith,*
hope, and love. But the greatest of these is love.

I know there is a place for me, pulled back suddenly
by the weight of something spoken, no longer
to the congregation, but to me. Someone, whoever,

cries out, the sad sound of a trumpet muted. And I look up
at the urn, empty, that will contain her as we each contain her.

Aubade to Childhood

(written senior year)

1.

something tells me Shakespeare
would never have gone by "Billy."

the name commands very little from adulthood
rolling as it does in small balanced somersaults.

2.

from years away
I hear children playing in the road
unscathed by the passing traffic
hitting tennis balls with aluminum bats
sending them orbiting off over foreign ground
over the neighbor's roof.

first, a bent ash
second, some collapsed hubcap
third, a stolen fluorescent cone
(it took three of us to carry it from the ditch).
I tagged each base as my brothers ran off
to find our ball on the other side of our world
and as the gravel spit itself
from under my running feet,
I hear them all calling my name out.
"Billy . . . Billy . . . Billy!"
I believed I could keep circling forever.

3.

my little sister is making a man
of our lawn, shaving it too close
and letting the dry soil cloud like the Midwest,
though we are far from there.

in sixth grade
I stole my brother's razor and pretended
to grow up. face to face to the mirror,
I trained my hand
to glide the razor against my smooth skin
with the grace of the lawnmower
disturbing the surface of the yard
but resolving nothing.

and I would have gotten away with it
but in the finishing moments
I grew impatient, drew my head and chin back
to nick my youthful skin.
it stung at first. then the blood
swelled against the lather
as if to boast at its escape.

and I rinsed my minor wound, cleaning nothing,
then ran from the bathroom to hide my face in a towel
until dinner.

4.

people ask me and I answer.

nothing is wrong with "William,"
perched on the line like a hungry bird.
but everything becomes devoured by maturity.

something dies and is buried
in the empty lot — a young bird —
and quiet comes to an empty house.
children play ball there
and curse over the sacred ground.

the other birds, amazed by the strange
displacement of a generation,
call to the children to come back outside
and play again under the estranged sun.

nothing is wrong with "William,"
I tell them, but why do things have to change?

5.

I once attempted to learn cursive,
a tangle of loops and circles. I finished,
unsuccessful, and waited, misplaced
among the settled rows of desks
for the teacher to come with her ruler.
maybe, I decide, I have remained
attached to my young name
because I would hate to have to learn another,
afraid of that illegible language of children.

6.

December was the shortest it has ever been
and the warmest. I remember
what we call "snow" in Florida,
though it melts impatiently as it falls earthward.

To celebrate, I did not rejoice in Christ's honor,
instead struggled to reconnect
to the visions of sugarplums I no longer dream of.
I spied from second-story mall railings
not on Santa, but on the children who worship him
then dart off like wild pigeons
still clinging to their mothers and fathers.

Christmas day, I too clung to a father.

David unwrapped more toys than I did
and I helped him test them,
drove down to a 7-11
to check the reception on long-distance
walkie-talkies. "Red Dog One to Blue Fox Three."
He came in loud and clear.

finis

The dawn is up. We wait at the dockside
since midnight. My 18th, threshold
of nothing really, but cigarettes and lottery tickets,
neither of which I celebrate,
and instead of parading down the lapped shore,
tightfisted and unruly, I have been calling my name out
to the water's edge for hours,
begging my youth to remain attached
to my branches like unripe fruit.
I hope I listen.

2. giving it wings

Sleepover

Saturday morning after any of Dad's late Fridays,
I snuck into the garage and found the red bucket
he had used to paint the house. I mixed the potions
from under the kitchen sink: Murphy's Oil, Pledge,
Windex, Tarn-X, Tilex — each with its own dizzy ghost.

What would my father have found if he was awake?
A boy pouring acids into his own miracle solvent
which, he must have imagined, would clean anything.
But all it was good for was taking the paint off the fence
and killing the grass where I finally gave up

and poured it out. When I was seventeen,
I attempted to take acid while sleeping over
at Ben's house. His parents weren't home
when he handed me a square of paper and told me
to put it on my tongue. I liked him, so I did.

He gave me a moment for the world to dissolve,
then kissed it out of my mouth. No pause,
no argument in my body as he pulled me onto the couch.
I think of the little boy giving up by the fence,
wondering if the grass will ever grow back.

Give It Wings

My first love poem — well, the first to a boy
that needed to be in secret — hid my love

in a cage. Cliché after cliché, singing.
I didn't stop until I had whole aviaries, love

coming out, everywhere and relentless.
I never thought it was Love, just

love, in a simple way that was safe
and easy to say because it meant nothing.

It wasn't long before I learned who not to say it to
and who not to feel it for, who not to write about

because if you give it wings, it wants to fly away.

Talking in the Dark

Before college, before high school, before my voice
finally cracked, before I could do my first pull-up,
and long before my first real kiss, you and I

held the same girls' hands. First Karen, then Tiffany,
then Jessica. And by the time you kissed Amy, I knew
it wasn't her I wanted to kiss. I spent the night at your house

and we talked in the dark until we fell asleep. Those years
were short ones, seem shorter now. I hated myself for lying
so still in the bed beside you, as awkward as a body

and as inarticulate. I have never wanted to kiss you,
only hold you now and then or be held. I know now
that you wouldn't have cared and just wanted to be

trusted. I have pictures of us with girls at dances.
I'm wearing my father's dress shirt. It balloons away
from my body. But you are right there next to me,

in my shirt's reach. Later you won't stand so close, and Amy
will have to pose us, pleading *closer. No, no. Closer.*

Cologne

It's the first day of my junior year and I'm new.
Because I look new and feel new, because you said
I should buy new clothes and I did. Who are you
but the first boy I kissed? First boy I wanted to
blame? I said tell me everything and you told me
everything you wanted me to know. Your father,
your far mother, bottles and bottles of beer. I said
I was sorry for them but you never cried in front of me
and I learned. You took my shirt off and had me
take off yours. It was nice to have you do it.
Undoing each other. You riffled in your bag
and took out your cologne, wanted to let me wear it —
I liked the smell, dizzying as you. Alcoholic at first
and then the evaporation. Who are you but
what all you gave me: first kiss, first more than kiss,
and your cologne? I sit in first period, smelling my wrist,
pretending you'll walk in. But by now you're at school
up north, forgetting me as your bottle runs out. And I know
I'm not the only one. Daniel and others are wearing it too.
But I can't be angry after everything you've changed.

This Bird Has Flown

1. Tightening

Who was it who told me the first thing
a child learns to do is hold? My father
would put his hand into my brother's crib
and Brian must have reached to curl
his five fingers around our father's one.

The first thing we learn to do is grasp,
claim, contain what is ours — or what we want
to be. When I was taught to tie my shoes
my father explained the mechanics of string
while my mother showed me again and again.

But when my brother kneeled to teach me,
taking my hands in his, I knew it was
something I needed to learn, listening again,
eyes affixed. I don't remember how many tries
it actually took, but I remember tightening

the one loop through the other and looking up
at him. I'm sure, now, his pride was more
about him being able to teach me than for me
having learned, but Brian smiled, stood, turned,
running to tell the world of me. Look

what my brother did and look what we did
together.

2. Listening Through the Wall

It's spring and Kurt Cobain has shot himself and my brother,
like so many brothers, locks himself in his room —

At night, after I've been tucked in, I peel the sheets off
and sneak into the bathroom, where I can listen

as he plays the guitar. I can't understand the lyrics — the music
changes as it trembles through posters and paint, makeshift dividers

of drywall, piping, and pine, toward me. And I am, myself, changed,
pulled by chords, shaken, into the dreamed room, where

we are still running away together, are still children, both of us,
    and he is
still wanting to share the world, string by string.

3. Patience

When his voice drops and he begins to shave,
my mother explains about a man's body,
how it turns from one thing into another.
I am slow, she tells me, as she was slow,
that I need to be patient, as she was. My father
tells me how my mother used to cry, her breasts
smaller than the other girls', not yet a woman.
When she tells me to be patient, I remember
how Brian would come home from school
before I was old enough to follow him there,
how he would be happy to see me, then.
Dancing together to the White Album,
before all music was his.

4. Conspirators

One evening, Brian and I ride together
in the back of David's truck and he confesses
one thing after another, like scarves pulled
from a magician's fist until, all of a sudden, he stops.
I'm younger and still afraid of drugs, so he's not quite safe
telling me any of this. But it's the first time
he has told me anything and I want him to trust me.
I don't have anything to tell him, not yet,
am a good boy with no secrets, except those
kept from myself. He's finally letting me into his life,
giving me that music and trust and a love
that has been slow, awkward, but always ours.

5. Thirst

The night I first kissed a boy, Brian sat with Dad
in the living room, talking. I left my room
for some water and the two of them were on the couch,
unaware. And I saw him there, how he looked up,
smiled as if he knew, though he didn't.
How late I thought it was when I rose from kissing,
thinking the house would be dark, the family
put away for sleep. But Brian was up, and so was Dad,
and I felt so young, turning the faucet on,
embarrassed by my thirst. I hurried back to my room,
where I must have seemed so awkward. I wanted
to tell Brian then, but he was loving me
for what seemed like the first time, and I wanted
to keep him close.

6. His Vanishing

Days of glaze I have brushed on, a sky blue
the teacher promises will fog, then go clear
in the kiln. And it does, so clear the big eye
seems watery and severe. There's one big horn,
scored deep with forged texture. I don't know
what I will do with it, so when I take it home
and Brian sees it and claims it for his bedroom wall,
I give it away, happily.

He's leaving, slowly.

Dad buys huge brown boxes. I help Brian
fold them, sitting in his room, listening
to him sing "Norwegian Wood,"
telling me what acid is like. Later,
a girlfriend of his who knows tells him
everything about me. He doesn't listen
and I thank him quietly for understanding,
for closing to her before closing to me,
not letting it take away from us.

We pull each neon star from his wall,
and I can't help but feel like I am participating
in his vanishing. Having lost so much already
in the sweep of self, I'm not ready to let him go.
But I don't tell him that or anything, not yet.
I let him leave, feeling my brother
doesn't know me, and never will.

Following

On a camping trip, my father and I
stepped away and followed the dark
to where a railroad track

cut through the trees. We followed
that path, belonging
not to us but to the machine

we would never see.
The way I remember it, we
collected fireflies in a gallon-

sized Ziploc bag, eight or
twelve at a time, and then
let them go. Unable

to tell them apart, we watched
as they, blinking, rose,
wearing only their tiny fire.

And then we'd find more,
hold them just long enough
to make them ours

before letting them go too.
That night, as we walked
along the tracks, listening,

at first, more for a train
than to each other, he told me
how he gave up

being an artist
to have a family. And I let him
stop there, end the story

and follow the rails back
to camp. It was the first time
I saw my father

open, as if to say *Don't
be me, I don't know everything.*
It was the summer I first

kissed a boy, first strayed
from what my father
wanted. I wanted

to tell him. There was
that long quiet, I thought
I was going to

assure him I was
happy. That long silence
when we both pretended

we heard something
racing at us through the dark.
I didn't know how

to tell him he was right,
things had changed and I was
different. He saw it in me —

there was a moment
when I was listening, right before
his story stopped, right then,

when I could have told him,
but didn't, and we turned
toward camp, nothing left

to say, and so much more
than air between us.

Cover

First it was boys your age who you liked. Jeremy
played the piano and softball and asked you
to stay over. You were in fifth grade, before sex

could possibly exist, so you looked at pictures
of women in magazines and were men, then,
together. And then it was boys who you didn't know.

In the locker room, Chris didn't wear his shirt
and you saw his shoulders. You weren't sure
why you started buying his brand of deodorant,

only that you wanted to run like him or, maybe,
alongside him. But later, you sort of know.
In that vague way you know you want to

write or paint. In that way you know you don't like
sweating. And, eventually, there is that first magazine.
Stolen in secret and hidden near your bed. Mostly,

you want to feel secure, defended by the existence
of others like you. It's not about their bodies as much
as that first kiss, how you see them hold each other.

That cover, they aren't ashamed.

Canon

Of course, it gets easier. But there is still that
occasional panic. Hungry, or even starved
for history, that sense of belonging, you
do a frantic search at the library. Keywords:

GAY or HOMOSEXUAL and POETRY or
WRITER and the screen distills the canon.
You pace by the aisle until it's empty, read
that anthology in a safe corner, embarrassed

by the cover, though there's really nothing
threatening about it. And then there are those
first loves: Auden, Doty, Whitman. They say
Here is the world. Here. It's yours and it's

all right. So you want to check it out, even
stand in line while your palms sweat
against the laminate, before you figure out
you have five dollars and thirty cents,

which is just enough to photocopy
the better third. So you step out of line,
hurry frantically until fifty-three pages
of their world are yours.

Smoking

Ed says he will stop smoking if I stop eating
meat and I say *sure*, but immediately think *No,
it's not the same — your killing yourself and my
killing poultry*. And I wonder if he quits for me,
will I be the one he's sneaking it from?

I think of my mother, years ago, watching her
sneak just one outside a theatre before a movie.
It was *our secret* and she knew I wouldn't dare
tell David or bring it up at dinner. I was ten
and couldn't have stopped her if I tried
but it still felt like my fault because I loved
having secrets with her and hungered for trust.

Eight years later, we'll sit across from each other
at breakfast and I'll want to hear everything I know
she won't tell me, so I can feel more normal.
My mother leans into a whisper, so close I can taste
the smoke off her breath, and says, *Billy*.
I smile and she says, *can you keep a secret?*
I hope for the worst — because the worst
makes me feel better — and she tells me things
so slight I can't remember them now.

Histories

I look at pictures of an invasion, black and white
and blazing, despite how the blacks have gone gray.
I rip out photographs from an old issue
of *National Geographic* — or rather pieces of each:
Love carved into a park bench, a woman's glove,
a swan, blurs of flags in the wind. The rivers
descending through the farm-green fields curve
like fractures of a jigsaw puzzle, bend back
toward themselves. The little poet I am
must be so angry. I don't know what I'm writing,
but I write and write in journals without lines,
so that I can spin the pages any way I want.
One poem goes up the spine while another dribbles down
in lines intended to be tears. I love the impressionists,
make galleries among poems for Renoir, mostly
because I love his name.

I look at the photographs' paused geography,
imagine how diligently the rivers must have worked
to curve back. We all want, in some way, to reach back,
to ourselves or where we descended, and whisper.
At one point, the caption explains, the Volturno River
nearly meets itself for a moment of reflection.

In my journal, I invent the rest: how hard earth must be
for the waters to never mix, how at times
the tidewater rises and the river swells as if to take over
that narrow margin. You can't help, I write,
but hear the concatenation of a river or a history.
Where did I find that word? I wonder
if I even knew what it meant. But who wouldn't love
the thought of standing in one place and drinking
from two generations of water? Reading it later,
I'll know why I was upset and will want to cry again

where I did, in the margin, for the boy I was
when I was fifteen and didn't know it was okay
to write or desire without metaphor. I dreamt I was nothing
but a kite's anchor, collages of men's faces,
makeshift buildings of paper. Years later
I'll wonder how I didn't know I was lonely
when everyone around me did.

Before

After I hear the rumor that you're gay. After I steal your number
from the office at school. After I shake by the phone and after

I finally do call and your father answers
And you, Michael, say *Come over.*

After your dad walks in on us — thank God not touching
or even on the same bed. We've been talking.

You've shown me a calendar you bought at Structure,
men in their underwear but as good as naked.

Your favorite is July because there the men touch each other,
arms over and around tanned shoulders. I was once scared

as you are, your kiss like a little confession, the calendar
something to hide where no one will find it, hold it

against you. After you hear their door shut, you lean
over me, press your mouth against my mouth.

After I kiss you back, you show your body off like a kid
who brings a gun to school, not knowing what it is

or that it's loaded. It's easy to say our breaths rushed out
like the breaths of two men racing, because to you we are

racing. But I don't know that. After your eyes roll back,
and you roll off me, and I roll onto you, you push me off,

saying that you aren't gay, that I made you do it.

A Subtle Shade of Blue

The day I met Ben, he told me a story
he claimed he had read about a man
who saw other men's sexual auras

giving off a blue light. Some would be
subtle, practically invisible and milk-white
as the sky after snowfall. Others

would beam out translucent but evident layers.
Regardless, Ben explained, the blues changed
as each day the men felt differently.

I have never believed in auras, wantonly blue
or otherwise, but Ben liked Ani and made me
a tape of Tori's B-sides, so I walked with him

to physics, listened to him as he went on.
I imagined the men he described, crossing
a busy intersection, wearing their particular shade

like the birthday presents Ben's mother
decorated for him, sheet upon sheet
of blue cellophane. I wanted to be

just what he wanted, a subtle shade,
discreetly and penetrably blue.

Look at Me

When I met you, I was already broken.
You were just another who wasn't sure.
After Michael, I still wanted a kiss
from someone who would mean it.

I called you twice a day for weeks.
A friend said you asked about me.
I thought, perhaps, she had made it up,
but you did ask and called me.

We were getting close. I went to your house
to stay the night. You had me
look at porn and fed me pot. Look at me,
I can't even admit I liked you.

Ben, you are so beautiful I'll cry for days.
But that night, you smoked me out,
put a square of paper on my tongue.
Look at me, trying to pretend I was innocent.

I knew what you were doing.
You told me I was your best friend
and I let you lie with me on the couch.
Your socks played at my ankles

as we lay there for a full minute, unsure.
But you knew what you were doing
as you kissed your acid off my tongue.
I felt nothing. You said it was coming on

so the two of us kissed until dawn.
We let our mouths speak to our bodies.
I smiled when you opened your eyes
and looked at me.

In the morning, you felt sick.
I went on to school while you slept.
All that day I said I loved you
to our friends, who asked where you were

while I said nothing, only waited
all day to get home and call you.
You answered the phone, but nothing else.

I thought that night would make you mine,
but I didn't know what you were doing.

On Remembering What I Wrote to You

I don't expect you to read this poem
or know, even, that I have written you poems

about the two of us in physics, learning,
instead, each other's loves — my learning yours

could never be me. If you knew I had waited
so long at the beach for you to meet me,

the whole time writing to you in the sand,
before you finally came, singing behind me,

I don't know what you'd think. It was red tide
and we coughed in the car on the way home, joking

that I had killed you by asking you to come there.

Teeth

I could say I remember the yard, lit from the street, clovers
turned constellations as we were spotted
by the motion detector. I could say I remember

Michael's voice as he pinned me between the dark
and my small car, the window's cold

licking my back through my shirt, his tongue working
its will against mine until I stopped opening
my mouth, all those moments until he stopped

also. Some boys want to kiss or be kissed like that.
Some boys want you to push their hair from their faces

and pretend to gaze into their eyes while some don't
know what they want. I don't know what
Michael wanted but I let him

kiss me. I wanted him to — like I want to say
I remember the reflection off the wet grass, the night's

million surfaces all shimmering and still.
But I don't remember anything but the dark
of his mouth, that hungry space between us. I hoped

something about the kiss would change me or him, some
unlit part of me would slowly ignite or gently

ease into fire, arms pulling him into me. But he kissed me
and I remember trying but giving up, the way Michael had tried
to kiss girls and felt nothing, the way a car door

is almost comfortable against your back, then isn't,
the way his mouth opened before his tongue

felt for mine, before it slid against my teeth, before
it, almost pleading, eased away.

Only Pretending

My senior year, I dated John and Michael
didn't approve because John gave him
dirty looks, and he should have —
Michael was always getting in the way,
making fun of him and his frail stance.
I laughed and hated that I was laughing.

John and I went to dinner and we talked
about our parents. For me, how hard it was
because I needed, more than anything,
for my family to be proud. And he wiped
the sweat from his glass with a napkin,
poured some of his Coke into my empty cup
and told me his story: rich boy with nothing
planned for his life but love and theatre,
someone to bring home. And that year
it was me, and his mother had me sleep
in a far room and gave me quick looks,
knowing only how hard it was for her.
She paced the hall between us.

The end of the year, John and Michael
both came to hear me read "Aubade."
John sat a row ahead of Michael and
just to the side enough that Michael could
watch him as I started. I loved John a little
when he told me how proud he was — Now
I can't help but feel he was only pretending.
Michael told me how John yawned
as I started, looked bored. I stood up
and walked to the podium, clutch of papers
like a boy coming home from first grade
to show his art to anyone who'll look.
I cried that evening in Michael's car,

the same four seconds of a song playing
over and over. Silly now. Most things
eventually are. But that night I let it matter
to me — how much Michael must have meant
to me, for me to let what he said matter.
Even then I knew what he was doing:
watching John while John was watching me.

Yes

My mother asks me and it seems years pass
before I answer. When I first kissed a boy, I told her
about him, explained where we'd go or at least half

of everywhere he would take me.
First she said it would be okay and that she loved me.
But I said *No*, said *He's just a friend*, laughed.

Then cried in the shower because she made me
lie to her. But I thought she was convinced
and, perhaps, so was I. Years before that,

she asked. *Of you and your brother,*
she said, *you'd be the one to get an earring.*
Wasn't that her way of testing the water?

I said *No* and argued about the feeling
of metal in my skin, how I would never

do something permanent to my body.
Before that, years and years before
I could possibly know what I was

asking for, she slid me a sheet of paper, asked
what I wanted for Christmas: a Ninja Turtle,
some watercolors, an Easy-Bake Oven.

And she didn't say no. I opened the box, smiling,
not knowing how many boys had asked for it

and got a football or a pair of skates. She asked me,
didn't she? And each time I said *No*
and wanted her to believe me, maybe she did.

So after I say, finally, *Yes*, she'll cry.
She's known, she'll say, since I was five

and I'll want to ask why
she didn't tell me sooner, but instead ask

if she's okay. And she'll give me that look
I've seen before. When I stepped
through the back windshield of her car while

playing on it. When I crawled out
of that hiding place and startled her.
It's a mother's look and a mother's look only. It says

How dare you and *It's okay* and *I want you to be
safe* and finally okay and finally conscious,

stepping toward me slowly, as if into
an ocean, she says *Yes*.

3½ Love Sonnets

1

Ben calls and you unfold
from your dream he says
I'm sorry for calling
so early
he says I thought
you should know that
I'm dying but you aren't
sure if you are truly lucid
so you just sit there
dumb in the dim room
of sleep-going-
to-wake while

he starts crying
you are the first boy

2

he kissed first
morning after
a long night
without sleep first

sober grope so
you can't save yourself
from feeling
like a first mistake

like a platform
onto which he

crawled up and from
which he has lost

his balance
you bend

3

a paper clip around
your finger he tells you what
he is going to do now drop
out of school quit
his job and move to new
orleans with some man you
have never met after months
without a word from him you
hear his voice
on the answering machine
and it comes at you
twice like the stutter
of a cd skipping
you erase it quickly

3½

realizing you have
let him go
even after he stopped
crying and you said voice
thick with sleep don't talk
like that it doesn't mean
you're dying.

3. to the living

To the Living

Listen, I am talking to you.
  —William Bronk

I am afraid for each of us, daily,
and often in more than one way —
I am afraid for us all.

Not because we are not careful
but because we are not safe. Living:
heating leftovers, searching to match

that unmatched sock, letting the mail pile up.
I am scared for each of us as we separate
the egg white from the yolk. Not because

we are out of reach but because we are
out of touch — I press a shirt,
though I don't know when I'll wear it.

I print a second copy just in case,
never thinking of myself
as sensible. But I worry.

I would know if something were to happen
to you. Wouldn't I? I would know
if you weren't all right.

That makes it easier, somehow.
The world is much smaller and I am
glad you are all still here — maybe not

around — but still with me.

What I Hope Dying Is Like

When I imagined my life leaving my body,
I could picture a clear and singular soul
taking flight, its shape nearly the shape of me,
but fogged through. I could imagine the ground
steaming as my body was given up, the very air
unendurably still. But if there is such a thing
as a soul inside me, I would rather it not
feel like I've left when I have left the world.

Instead, I would like to become connected
to the life of each thing I finally touch.
One energy, not drawn out or transformed
but reaching from my life to the living ground
to the grass or cat or man, flooding the world
like it has been waiting to surge out. If I could feel
that first swell, the sensation leaving my skin
and taking in the senses of the grass and then
that first other animal. The first other person,
living nearest to my unloving body, feeling them too.
If I could still feel as each thing that feels
is braided by touch. That could be heaven,
knowing all along that touch was there,
knowing that death is only failing
to ignore it any longer.

Still

Walking home a month after your call, I passed the mural
beneath the overpass, its edges sketched and still
a ghostly white. Thinking of you, how your hands felt
through the sleeves of your sweater as I led you out

to the beach, your eyes closed, I looked at all that was left
unfinished and wondered how soon the artist would return
with her ladder and boxes. But it had been so cold lately
and I didn't know if she'd be back at all before spring.

And when I was almost home, rounding the corner, I saw,
among gray-green and the half-light, a single flower
still opening, momentarily and shockingly white. I bent
to pull it up, press it in a letter to you. But of course I didn't

reach it, and of course there was no letter. The winter was still
turning on, your life already sketched, finished but not complete.
I thought of how you laughed when you stepped into the sand,
how you didn't open your eyes until your feet were in the water.

The World, and More

The tide in, the foam alive
with the labor of carrying things in,
I park alone and look out
to as far as my headlights reveal:
textured gray of macadam, jeweled
near-white of sand and debris,
discreet shoreline, fixed distance.

Of course it is too dark to see
any horizon, but I know it's there
with continents beyond it. The world,
and more, further and further
past my headlights' minor reach.
This is what we have in college, now:
a longer drive to the ocean, more time
to read, and an empty space where
we each were in one another's lives.

In high school, I drove Ben to Blockbuster
and let him pick one movie
he thought I needed to see. It was *Bent*
and we popped popcorn and curled up
like true friends and I watched him
as he watched the two men
haul rocks from one pile to the other,
then back. Sitting here, I think of him
as the waves roll things up out of the ocean
just to pull them back again.

I don't know if Ben knew he was
showing me what love could be,
however briefly, as I watched him
watch the two men making love
without touching. I'm not sure

why I blame him for being positive,
but I can't blame him for running away,
striving to live in whatever world
isn't caught by the light.
I would seal off, close myself
by opening the world.
I'm out on the waves, blind
and being rolled by what sounds
like millions laughing. Can you feel
without touch? Can you really?

Watching him then, I wanted
so badly to hold him.

What the Body Allows

One of my earliest whole memories — whole, I say
because I know it happened and know I remember
without being reminded — is of stepping away

from my mother at the beach, wandering
into the shallow surf and being frozen by fear.
The water rushing past me, between my ankles,

seemed so much like being pulled into the ocean.
I remember that fear: the heart raging against my chest,
my voice surging out without being summoned

by breath. I believed I was being taken, not to die,
but away. Even as a boy I knew what the body allows
isn't love, and that the body is an instrument, as the cello is.

As the bow is. There is not only one way to love,
I know that. Walking through a museum, alone, I count the pairs
that are searching together. Beauty, I fear, is fleeting.

Not because that is what I've been told — though it is —
but because I've held the feeling of being carried away
without a breath or a reason. I wrote Ben a poem

the morning he called. And though I never sent it to him,
I know he cried, as I had wanted to for him,
afraid of being taken, even if not to die.

A Dream for a Boy

As a child, I discovered a river lined in iridescence.
Was it my father who told me about Peru? Tumbes
is famous for her oysters. Looked over, my river
hid in a bed of mackerel-blue and pewter.

There weren't only shells. There were sapphire tiles,
cinder blocks and gems of glass rubbed smooth
by sand and the water's insistence. Detritus,
I imagined, of Floridian hurricanes —

the insides and outsides of homes along the Gulf,
forced open and hollowed like oysters displayed
with the coast's half-shells. The ruins were vast,
full of little, beautiful things and wholly mine.

I would have liked to take you there,
teach you to skip stones and realize the treasure
of a place to be alone when you need to be,
a place to find the world when you've lost it.

It is easy to dig in the remnants, skip the treasures
across the tumbling field of water, and forget
that the piece was a part of a whole. But the truth
is harder. When I told my dad about the ruins

I had scavenged for pearls and jewelry, he laughed
and turned my river into the Intercoastal —
turned my ruins into junk wedged in sand
to solve the scare of night erosions —

the same way the water had worked
away each night at the red bricks, turning them
into thin, smooth honeycombs, beautifully
unrecognizable, but so much less than the boy's dream.

Prayer for a Son

I am writing this to you because I have given up.
Love went first, and with love, sex. So with love, you.

I would have loved to hold you, hope for you
to love me as I do my father, free of reprieve.

I'd tell you the things we don't tell our children
and don't know why we don't, and teach you

the things my father taught me: how to eat like a man,
leaning over the sink so that you won't have to clean up

afterwards, how to hold, apologize, and forgive.
How to let go. This doesn't mean I don't love you.

I do. But I could never love anyone
like I do you. I hope you can forgive me that much.

Shaving Poem

In high school, I read a poem about us —
But it was a father and he was dying.
We are not this poem, now. I know that.

The son shaved his father, who just sat back,
life-heavy and open. We think of every storm
as Shakespearean. If there is traffic in the air

we sit around and wait for trouble. Pine needles
have been falling all afternoon. I think
there was a knock at the door, but it's only

a pinecone, hitting the roof of a car outside.
When you finally do knock, we sit and talk.
You tell me about the play you're in

and how you need to shave your head
for just one joke in some role.
I listen, mainly, and breathe

— not like breathing should be, but like it is
in poems: a conscious taking in of air,
a holding on, a driving out.

You ask if I will be the one
to do it. You've even brought a razor and a hat.
I wonder if you planned this moment:

the two of us on my porch one windy afternoon
after lunch. I know we are both sons, though
neither of us the other's father, but it is

how open you are as I cut the hair away,
how much you trust me with you, when maybe
you shouldn't. I remember so clearly the face

of the man in the poem, the rhetoric of a son
shaving his father — But I have to struggle to imagine
what has just happened, how glad I must have been

when you were finally at the door,
how you stepped in as if just out of the rain,
and sat as if at your own place at my table.

I don't know if there is something
you want to pass on, but there is something
you want to give me. In a few years,

I will remember as clearly as a poem
the way your hands felt your white scalp.
The way you reached first for your hat, then keys,

then me, before I let go and you drove away.

My Father, Reading to Me

I was so angry when I heard she told,
not because you knew, but because I wanted to
be a man before I stopped being a man to you.
And when Brian said that you were mad
that she did, that you knew and wanted me to
tell you, I pulled the book I was reading
up over my face so he couldn't see.
And when I opened my eyes to the text,
I looked at the strange shapes of the letters
and imagined you reading to me
like I have never remembered: me in your lap,
your finger tracing the page as you would
the spine down a woman's back.

Back to Life

It makes perfect sense, in one way, that worth is forged
from what the world allows that is rare. One by one,
my friends got tested after Ben called each of us.

One by one, they came back to life. I sit in my room,
gluing pictures into my journal, pretending I am young
and safe in my youth. I read poems about men in tiaras

that jewel the world into splendor. Some glitter here,
some brightening there, they pretend, and there's beauty.
My friends and lovers have become characters, each

with recognizable roles. One is fun, another is older
and makes me feel mature. Another needs me; another
I need. I had a dream that Ben was alive. He glowed

a deep blue while onstage, not unlike an angel.
And I smiled, though I knew I would wake up
and he would be dead again — the dream had not

given me that much. I woke and sat up in my bed
as I had the morning he first called, thinking of my dream
and how he looked, wrapped in light. And not until

halfway through breakfast did I realize he was alive
all along, that I had killed him in my sleep.
Let our lives be what's precious in this world,

even if it isn't always what is most rare.
Let us know each other's roles and decide
that that's not all we are to one another.

A Later Innocence

Remember how your skin grew
over a splinter too deep to remove.

Can the body really forget, as I do
with time? How much of my body

is the body I had when I was
first touched, first touching?

It's summer and I'm home
and don't know what to say to Michael

when I see him. What is left
to be said? My home is not mine now

as I visit it. Michael has gone on
without me. He says there's nothing

better to do and has convinced me
to go. The club is quite a drive,

but there is so much that needs
to be said, so much catching up.

The car seems like a perfect vehicle
for conversation: two people with nothing

but a small space to fill with voices.
I want to tell him how strange it feels

to only visit your home, looking out
past the trackless black of night,

motel neon off, like a star, in the distance.
But there is some beauty in visiting, dreaming

into the vacant rooms of the motel as we pass:
the emptiness of drawers and cabinets, hangers

unclothed and all too ready
to wear whatever, everything

disposable wrapped loosely in paper,
wanting or waiting to be taken,

unwrapped, disposed of.
Isn't that why I've come along:

to revel in the illusion of vacancy,
forget for the moment the weight

of living, each motion separate
from desire and impossible to name?

We're here before I've said anything.
Once we're inside, nothing can be said at all.

Pietà

Ed throws pennies in the street and says
he is making luck. I found, in the road,
what I thought was a ring. It was

only a bottle cap so I'm still not sure why
I put it in my pocket. He came to town to visit
and read his poetry to me. We went for coffee.

I sat across the table from him, bent
a paper clip into the shape of a heart and put it in
the ashtray while he smoked another.

He told me what really scares him
isn't just HIV, being defined by what's lacking
in your blood, but, of all things, having to tell his mother.

When he first got tested, after we found out
about Ben, he tried to write a poem
to put a shape to his fear. *Pietà*. He read to me

about Christ's body. I wasn't sure
if he would be able to finish as he spoke
of the Holy Mother, her closed eyes swelling,

her hands shaking as she felt for the last traces of life
in his body. I don't remember if he didn't finish writing it
because the test was negative, or if he didn't know

how to end it. I didn't tell him everything
I wanted him to know: how hard
the lines broke, how quickly he read

to the end, how I still hadn't been tested, so
had nightmares where my mother tucked me in
and cried over my dying body — she folds and refolds

the hem of the sheet and mumbles
that everything will be okay. She lights a candle,
rocks forward in that way small children do.

The worst part is before I figure out I'm dreaming
and she says to wake up. It's like the moment
you're alone in the dark and it occurs to you

that you might need to run — but you can't
get your legs to move. I don't tell him that, or how
I was almost home when I put my hand in my pocket

and found the bottle cap searching
through the cloth for my leg and, wondering why
it was there, tossed it back into the road.

Gift

Not very long after I meet Dan, it is summer
and he takes me to the part of the beach
where he comes to read. He tells me how he drives here
nights he needs to be away and we walk
across the rocks to where he sat the night
he stayed until dawn before driving two hours home.
            We sit on the ledge of graffiti
listening to waves tearing into the tide wall.
Of course we don't notice the loose rock
pulled from the rest, but in ten years,
I want to tell him, the whole place
could be carried away. But so will we.
What is really keeping us here? He tells me
of the night it was so cold he never left
his car. Instead, he parked close enough
to watch the violent spray. The car shivered
and bass hummed as the music rose
with the water. He tells me it changed everything,
hearing violins and electric noise as the ocean grew
too big for the shore.
            I want a place where I can come to write.
I want a parking lot close only to the ocean. I tell him
I need to find my own piece of the world
and he tells me I can have his. We can share it.
I tell him I want my own but
what I really mean is *Thank you.*

She Predicted You

I don't want to believe a future can be read,
but Ed says *She predicted you* and I become uncomfortable,

smiling as he explains: *It was my turn and she told me
someone in my life would teach me about myself*

in ways I couldn't. I think of the boy I was
and the last girl I dated, how she claimed she knew

my future. She smiled and I knew she was wrong
— bent over a cup of tea, reading the leaves.

She said *I see children, a woman and a white dog.*
And I smiled too, forgiving her for reading herself

into my life, loving her for what she had tried
to give me, and now, thankful Ed has told me.

Thankful she has read him and from her, he reads me.

Sudden Arrangement

1.

I've been alone
for so long and been content
to only witness love — the way a child witnesses
the sudden arrangement Easter morning,

climbs on the counter to where the lilies are
with only half their flowers open.
Because I've been happy without
love, without a kiss when I could

need one, or because I am spending
mornings awake and alone while friends are waking,
just now, with others or each other, kissing
toward feeling alive —

I have tried to find the feeling
on my own, in myself and the world,
not unlike the way the child opens
the unopened flowers, unwilling to wait.

2.

Tonight the stadium is empty and we've snuck in
to sit together in the big bowl of bleachers, looking up

to see if the sky looks any different with such a space
cleared and lit for our being. A week ago, I wouldn't have dreamt

of being here with anyone, let alone you, who I've only just met.
Tonight seems like a gift, not from you, but somehow

taken and held by both of us. Greg, I don't really know you,
but we've spent hours talking over coffee, driving around.

We don't say anything about how much we like each other.
Instead, only how upset Dan will be, since he likes you.

The stadium is so quiet around us, it is hard to believe
there is a world outside of this. There isn't

a single thing I would like more than to kiss you here.
But I don't and you don't either. We talk and talk,

our backs against the bleachers, voices rising together,
before walking back to my car, driving you home

and wishing there were a way to arrange this
so that no one would get hurt.

4. work

October

Yes, I will take you as a present. It is coming on
autumn, and I think it would be nice to keep you
warm through winter. Imagine how the branches will flower

outside my window, what each morning could look like
from my arms. What we have here now is not
what we could. Not yet. I lie in the grass on campus,

reading and staring up into the magnolias. The ground
is cold. I want you next to me. What do we have here
that isn't somewhere else? Studying together,

you ask about my religion. I tell you about the slow turn
of the world, how the Earth is made of earth, and how I prayed
when I was younger, bargaining for little miracles.

You ask about my family. I tell you about tin cans
filled with photographs, boys in the driveway
waving goodbye, the younger waiting and waiting

for his father. I draw a map of my life, draw stars
where each parent's house was, squares
where we ended up. You ask about art; I read a poem.

You ask about love; I read another.

Confession

I used to think I could never love a man
as I could a woman. Only men's bodies

could get me there, while it took a woman's voice
to calm me. Have I ever heard a man

sing a lullaby? I'm sure now that I have,
but once I wondered if I could trust a man

to love me as I wanted to love and be loved:
honestly and entirely. I've slept for hours

pressed against you, dreaming of nothing,
and have loved each waking since. I've gone

to work and thought, all shift, of the sweetness
of your laundry. You've left messages

on my machine at home, drunken and confessing
how you've been waiting to kiss me, embarrassed

by how quickly you miss me and how much.
When I get home, I find your voice begging me

to call, no matter how late, promising you
only want to sleep beside me. I call

and you curl along the line
my body makes as we lie there.

I will play your message over and over
as you sober. You may think it was for you

but it wasn't. I didn't erase it for months.

Sketch

To let myself love a man was once failing.
Because it would be allowing myself something
I knew I wanted. And then I did and was pushed away.

But there is no guilt here. I am loving you
over and over and without end. When you kiss me,

I don't think of love. I don't think at all, only taste
and smell: honey on bread, metallic cologne.
I hardly notice you at all. The first time I touched you,

you shuddered — not as if you were cold, but as a hand does
when reaching for something it has wanted so long

to touch — and not as if you were afraid,
but as the heart does, knowing what it touches
it won't want, ever, to let go.

Secrecy

It was at his dorm and I was waiting
for him to get dressed or finish playing
a video game. Or we were in my car
driving to Dan's house or the mall
or maybe sitting in my living room
drinking beer. Where were we
when he first told me that he read
in an article somewhere that peeling
the labels off of bottles is a sign
of sexual frustration? We laughed
and I said that I wasn't, kissed him,
perhaps, or touched the back of his neck
with my thumb or wrist. He smiled.
So when we are at a party, and I don't
know all of the people, we're not sure
if it will be okay to kiss or even touch.
So I make sure he sees me pretending
to peel the paper away from the cold
glass. And if that isn't enough, I tear
it off completely and hand it to him
and we sneak away into a hallway
or bathroom for a quick moment
of affection. I don't like the secrecy
but I guess it's exciting. At Dan's
Halloween party we don't have to
act straight, but we feel bad kissing
in front of him, so we go upstairs,
lock the door, and knock a painting
off of the bathroom wall. We don't
know which way is meant to be up
and finally decide how it should hang.
But of course we find out we were
wrong. I don't like the secrecy
but I guess it's exciting. At Greg's

friend's Halloween party, Mark
is decked out in Army gear. Greg
thinks he looks hot and I joke
that he must be gay, the way he
keeps staring at Greg. I don't know
anyone, so I must be quiet. I can
feel the looks; Mark is appraising me.
I think it's all in my head, do I really
see traces of his face paint on Greg?
No, of course not. But Mark does
accidentally knock a button off
of Greg's tuxedo and the world
gets smaller and smaller around me
until there is only me at one end
and Greg at the other.

A World, in Two Parts

1.

The season embodies the swell
of the gulf — its jewels are as swift
and mercurial as weather. I go

barefooted down the swollen dock
and find at the end of its tether
a catfish, gray with enormity, exactly

what I needed. *Why did you tell him*
you loved him? Because I did, still do.
I never said I loved him like that.

I'm amazed I can lift it from its world —
its whole weight is relentless and trembling.
So you loved him like a friend — then why

were you so upset when he left you
for Mark? We had talked about it before.
We both knew that he would want to eventually.

He snaps as I wrestle the hook out, struggles
as I elbow onto my chest, lower him
back into the water. *So it wasn't a surprise.*

No, it was a surprise that he thought
all of that made it okay. I let go,
expecting he will dart away, race into the dark.

Instead, there is a pause, a breath
in which I imagine he believes me
to be his savior, then he surges away.

2.

*You told him later that you just missed
having a boyfriend. Did you say this to hurt him?*
No. I said it because it was the truth.

But I hoped it would hurt him. *Did it?*
I pressed my hands to the glass
of a huge aquarium, dreaming my way

into the tank. *Did it?* I just wanted him
to talk to me. *What would you have wanted
him to say?* That he was sorry.

Didn't he apologize? No, sorry he didn't
try to hide the fact that he was choosing
someone else. Sorry that he didn't hesitate.

The fish were foreign and impossible
guests — a conjured lexicon of gems:
betta, tetra, oranda, koi. Evidence

of a world only seen from the outside.

From Breaking

At the beach, when Brian and I would go with Dad,
the two of us stood together in the surf, kicking and kicking
at the waves. What children we were

to pretend we believed we could keep them
from breaking. What children we were to believe
our will had any power over a body

so much greater than ours. When Greg first said
it wasn't working, I didn't cry until he offered me his necklace
and then it didn't stop. I said I didn't want it

and we went to Denny's and sat at opposite ends of the table.
He tried to read me with a distant compassion
while I stirred my root beer with the straw,

imagining faces in the slow traffic passing
a bad accident, staring, not knowing what to look for or why.
I thought of the will of children as I twisted and twisted

the straw wrapper into a knot, not wanting to talk,
not wanting to listen. What was it my brother called out
over the ocean? Years later, I can't help but wonder

why we pretend to believe.

Because

Because you let your necklace know
the slopes of my shoulders. Because now you let him
wear your necklace.

Because of your height and where my arms went
when I held you. Because I didn't know
that would be our last kiss. Because you aren't
careful with me. You think of me
when you're with him.

Because the room is only half-full; the bed
is half-empty. Because I'm tired
of getting so much sleep.
Because you dreamt of snakes
the night we first slept apart.
Or because I peel labels off bottles.

Because you can still tell me your dreams.
Because you whimper when you have to
take medicine — but I make you anyway.
Because you make faces
that tell me everything. Because we agree
that lovers should be friends.
Because you don't dream of him.

Because you haven't read the books you borrowed.
Because your clothes are still on hangers
in my closet. Because I save your phone messages.
Because I am afraid you will give away
everything that is ours. Because I'm not
getting any better at this.

Work

1.

The weekend after we broke up I couldn't go to work
because I knew the people would ask how you were
and I didn't want to tell them. You weren't
with me anymore. I didn't want to see them.

The next weekend I couldn't go in either
because I knew I couldn't smile for people
and I knew I wouldn't make any money
and I knew I would be waiting for you to come in.

The weekend after that I tried to go in
but the manager asked if I wanted off,
so how could I stay? I clocked out
and sat in a back booth and read.

2.

I never said I loved the grammar.
I said I loved the words you use —

ordinary language, but something
about the vowels. I don't remember

crying, really. Why should I?
It isn't like we were no longer

friends. I told my mom
about you and him. She said

it wouldn't last, but I still
wished you both the best.

3.

I'm over you. But I saw a guy
in the paper that looked like you
and I thought I'd call just to see —
When did you change

your answering machine message?
I heard it and thought I heard him
laughing through the white noise.
It was only then that I knew

there will always be somebody else
who doesn't work as hard as you
but makes more money.

Soundtrack

You told me how much there was
that you wanted to say but couldn't.
So for Christmas you burned me

two CDs — one with music
you thought I'd like, and the other
filled with things you thought

I should hear. You tucked a letter
in the case. I locked myself in a room
to read it. Your instructions:

listen to it alone and all at once.
You explained how it would tell me
the things you were wanting to say.

I waited until my roommate had left

"Hey, Man"

and laid on the futon in the living room, the world
tightening around my throat, like one loop
of a shoelace encircling the other, until I was
off the futon, my back against the hardwood floor,
closer to the speaker, as easily parallel to heaven
as hell. I have so many questions to ask you,
but this is all the answer I have.

"Ain't That the Way"

By the second track,
you told me you loved me.
I still wasn't crying,
my body curling

into itself as the disc
spun in place, calling.
Think of how a planet circles
its small sun.

"The Middle"

I don't want to underestimate it. I know it takes time.
One friend says to dive into work. Another knows
that's just how I got here.

"Relating to a Psychopath"

I felt bad each time I called. Even while we were dating
I would pace by the phone, wondering

if you would be annoyed or begin to get tired of me.
You did and are still

making me pace, months later.

"Shadows"

As a child, I could see
faces in wood grain, cities
full of families and dark fur

in stucco, linoleum or brick.
If the paint was peeling there was a story
in the shadowed distortion.

Rorschach's twisted children
laughed at the clowns in the living room;
Care Bears rode on clouds

along the bathroom floor. I guess
I haven't stared at a surface
for as long since. The ceiling

seems to know your name.
The walls know how to spell it.

"Beautiful Way"

I remember: your alcoholic breath
the night you left your message,
how you whispered into my ear
even though no one was home to hear,
vodka-laced kisses at Dan's house,
his couch, your tuxedo, the whole room
dizzy as now, only your face clear.

"Trouble"

I think this is where I cried.
I was waiting and waiting
for you to say you were sorry
for ending us, that you were stupid
and unkind.
                    Piano crooning,
its slow bass humming like a car wreck.
I felt it ticking through the floor
and imagined myself in the box
being struck among the chords.

"Long Walk"

That first night we stayed up together until almost dawn,
after watching Alice play at a coffee shop.

You sat with her boyfriend and I sat behind you,
watching you turn, every couple minutes, just enough

to look at me. Those early looks were my favorites.
You didn't seem to know exactly what you were doing

and gave me more than you knew. We talked that night,
surprised, we said, we hadn't met sooner.

"Got 'Til It's Gone"

We watched Alice sing at a restaurant.
You requested "Big Yellow Taxi,"
and, after, ran across University Avenue
to buy candy at the gas station: Sour Skittles,
because you liked the red ones. Greg,
you're such a child — I think that's why
I loved you the little you let me. You smiled
at kids as they stared at how tall you were.
And when they smiled back, I knew
I was safe with you. I thought of children
on your shoulders made tall as giants
and decided there was a future — yes, for us,
but also a future for me.

"How to Disappear Completely"

I wish you would
call me. I wish you would
talk to me, explain.
I wish you knew
me, how I only need
a word and a wish
of love. I wish you
knew what I wanted
and could see I'm not

something to fear.
I wish you could see
why I love you
and how little.

"Resolution"

Alice comes home and asks if I'm all right.
I think of the night you and I met her for dinner,
sat her down as one would a child and told her
what we had heard about her boyfriend.

Later, you asked what I would do
and were so happy when I said I would leave you,
because my insistence implied my loyalty.
I thought there was a safe place —

Maybe there is, but I thought that place
was somewhere between your ear and shoulder.
Alice looks at me when she asks how I am
and I think of the night we told her,

how she didn't seem surprised. I'm sure, now, she was.
I imagine her anger, take it in, put it on. I build myself
a room with your infidelity. But, of course, you weren't —
how can I call it infidelity if you dumped me just before?

I watch my hand rise to wipe my cheek, my sorrow
seeming less and less legitimate, until all I can do
is fall into her. I don't remember, but maybe
she'll remind me how, shaking, I answered.

Boxes

It was the week before Christmas break
and I had made you a box, found all sorts
of little things of yours, decided to give them

back: a CD you lent me, a shirt and some boxers.
I brought it over one night, set it on your bed
next to things Mark had given you, and was happy

that I didn't cry in front of you. I didn't
give you everything, couldn't bring myself to take
your picture off my mirror. There are a lot of things

I never told you. The night I found a shirt of yours
that still smelled like your cologne, I let it
lay across your pillow next to me,

though I knew I shouldn't. I started
another box — one full of things I would give you
when we got back together. The stuff I found

that reminded me of you: stickers for bands
you liked, labels, a cowboy cut from a magazine —
looking back, there was nothing there but paper

you wouldn't really want, so it's okay
that I threw it away. I was trying so hard
to fill your box, but by that time I was tired

and had given up on you.

December

I am visiting my family when I think of you,
Dan, and want to think of coasts that sprawl
so far you cannot map them, the turbulence
of wind against a fast car. I want to write
as if we paused at that tide wall long enough
for you to really have given it to me.
Instead, I think of beer, of dancing in dark
rooms when we think someone is watching,
of long nights we've stayed up talking
about Greg and how unfair that must be.
I didn't know you liked him. I knew a little
but didn't let myself believe it. And what I did
know about him didn't seem real and you didn't
seem to take him seriously. And that makes it
my fault. I hear you drove for hours the night
you found out. I hear you got drunk the first time
you saw us together. But I didn't hear it from you,
which makes it worse because it makes you good
while it makes me so bad. I'm sorry you drank,
so sorry Greg and I held each other in your house
and with you there. I don't feel better
and don't really want to. There are things we do
when no one's looking that make us feel
like we're alive. And when we're finished
we want to die — not for what we've done,
but for only feeling when no one's there.

Your Opening

It was about the secrecy. Mark wasn't out
and so you wanted that quick kiss in the dark.
It was about his masculinity and I made myself
all right with that. At least then it wasn't about

how often I called or how badly I missed you.
We went to Denny's, just you and I, finally.
You talked about your sex and I listened, unable
to look at you. Because it could mean imagining him,

his hands sweeping away any trace of me.
I don't know how long it's been since we've talked.
Really talked. So when you call to see
if I still have your cuff links from Halloween,

at first I am a little startled by your voice, then
by how unstartling it is to hear you. I turn
in my chair and see the little box that holds them,
its black velour dusty. I think of the things I gave you

back, how I left this little box on my shelf
intentionally, so you'd have to call to get them.
I waited, but finally forgot all about them.
You explain how Mark is going to wear your tuxedo

to some opening of yours. I laugh, since he is
a good half-foot shorter. And you laugh too,
saying *I know, but he doesn't care*. He's going to
wear it, regardless. I didn't even realize I was smiling

as I talked to you about him. I didn't even know
how happy that had made me. If your love is real
and separate from me. If Mark is funny and charming
and sweet. I can be happy for you and we can be okay.

Apologia

If we had a place that was ours, wouldn't it be that stadium, that
    floodlit dream
of a place, with its rows and rows of emptiness? Sure, we could claim

so many other places. That month, and since, we had filled so much
    of the city
with ourselves and our tired, relentless matters. Dan's couch, where
    we lay

drunk together, your room or mine, a club we let ourselves be
    coupled in?
But I haven't been alone with anyone like that first night, since.

So much of the city ours, so much of it filled by our love's brevity,
if only because there didn't seem to be anyone else

desiring to fill it. So there we were, filling an unfulfilled evening, and
    here we are
barely friends and hardly in touch, though I like to believe we both
    would rather be.

I said *tell me the truth* and then held it against you. I said *treat me like
    a friend*
and when you did I felt betrayed, if only because I wanted to be
    called more often

than a friend would be. If I said *I'm sorry*, I know you would
    forgive me.
If I said *I know now how hard you tried — forgive me*, I know you
    would.

But what I really want is to give it all back, everything. Give back
    my birthday,

not because Dan and you ended up covered in cake. I'd give you
    back

New Year's, and not because we were both there and didn't kiss, and
    Christmas,
not because I was working so hard to have you back — rigged that
    bag of Skittles

so they'd all be red. I would give you back all that time I didn't know
    how to give you
away. I'd even wrap up Halloween in a little box of candy and hand
    it back to you,

that one holiday we were together and I was happy. And there we
    would be,
the two of us in the stadium, deciding where to go next. If we had a
    place,

wouldn't that be it? That first place where we did nothing wrong.

Anatomy

Think of the body as a body
of smaller masses and those masses
as groups of cells, each piece smaller

than you, each division worth tracking.
Think of the body as something that works
all day and all night for you.

Think of your body as something that needs
food and water and touch. Suddenly
the world is smaller

and each cell is so big if only because
it is easy to predict, while the world is
so hard. Think of your body

as something that needs warmth:
that hand on your back
when you don't expect it, that lip

against your cheek, that neck next
to yours. If you recognize you need
tension and release and then more

tension. If you think of your body
as smart, your heart as a muscle
that thinks, as all of you thinks, then

suddenly the world is smaller and less
difficult to live in. It is okay to cry, okay
to miss someone who has hurt you,

okay to love or not to love. Your body
is thinking, telling you to just let go.
Listen, your heart is beating —

Step back into the world.

5. coming into adagio

Looking Back

1.

Walking today, a bird ahead of me
twisted its body in the amber light,
lifted itself into the air and, as if
someone or something else was out of sight
doing the work of lifting, glided up
and arched above me, tethered to my stare,
over my body and behind, away.
I turned to look and there was nothing there.
No leaf, no shadow settling, nothing.
That's it. I could say I thought of Greg — my bird
had rushed, like him, into and from my life.
But I didn't think of anything, only heard
and stood and watched it learn of me and go.
That's it. I looked at life and not the sorrow.

2. Darkroom, Accidental

Everything red — everything, even shadows
blood-dark, the room seemed scared of light.
We covered prints as owls would swathe their nests
and were artists in our artificial night.

I'm walking home. The CD skips. I swear
she meant to sing *Oh Lord above!* But no,
the glitch corrects. She sings *Lo-ve*, again
and again. I think of how I once exposed

the paper twice and how the image rose,
shadows upon each other. In the print,

two boys appeared to kiss, twinned lovers joined
at the mouth. It was a tender kiss. But I bent,

blushing among the safe-lights, and let it burn.
There was a day I'd cower from a kiss,
but now I'm walking home with such a gesture.
Lo-ve, Lo-ve, Lo-ve. The song insists.

3.

Love brings you hope, purpose, and resurrection.
And though you say you're not religious minded,
you want to have faith in something daily yours
that brings you joy. What is existence, really,
but the product of one's own belief? If we
can name it, if we have given it a place
inside us, how could it not be there? Name
one thing more possible, more durable,
more real than people. It is not naive
to recognize existence, something you aren't
sure of — it is naiveté to ignore
the possibility that something might.
Go. Look directly back at it. It will
still be there. Dare to let the world look back
at you. If we give love a space, a name,
ourselves, there is no end to what we see.

Ginger

Visiting home — how strange it still is to say that,
and how real — I saw Ginger sleeping
beneath the coffee table. Remembering

how she wandered into our yard,
how we tied her up out back and wanted,
so badly, to keep her, I lower myself

slowly so that my face is even with hers
but perpendicular. Looking so closely, I know
I still don't love her. She's been here so long

her gold has gone gray. I would like so much
to need her, to look into her eyes and find a depth
that proves she knows me. We've watched each other

grow. But she is not what a person is
in my life, has already forgotten why
she came to stay here. I remember wanting her

so badly. But now, watching her sleep,
I imagine what the family will say when she goes —
will they call me or wait for me to call? Will I come to visit

and take days to notice? They'll say *Yes,
she's finally run off*. She'll have died,
remembering nothing.

The World, Without Us

1. First Death

The year my grandfather died, I was given a fish
for my birthday. Red body, silver gills. I don't remember
what I named him, but he was all fire and ice. Captured

by the flick and flow of his fins, those thin sheets
that were shockingly a part of him, I watched him pace
in his bowl, as my brother and I did in our yard,

searching and searching as if there was something more
in those six inches of water. Like a comet or a fire engine
passing, he was — and then, suddenly, wasn't. One morning,

I went to feed him, and he was gone. I was learning
the states of matter in school, asked my dad if my fish could
evaporate into the air with the water. He didn't answer,

just looked at my mother, who only turned back to the sink,
having flushed him earlier, not wanting me to see that dulling
and swelling body, knowing I knew as much as I could

about death, not wanting me, ever, to know it, only what it was.

2. Fort

We built it for the four of us. By August
it was the one of me — trying in vain
to read, I'd fall asleep five feet above
the ground. No one around, not even Brian.
Winter and I, too young to work or leave,
climbed up the ladder, hoping I could hide

in the woods, not knowing who I was
avoiding.
                                January and alive
like nothing in the woods — even our fort
was dead inside and rotting from beneath me.
Too young to know the wood had softened — not
afraid of death and less afraid of dying,
I climbed towards loneliness and found the ground,
no one at home, not even Brian around.

3. In Summer Here, It Rains Each Afternoon

. . . so that you might step inside and be cooled and refreshed,
and less yourself than part of everthing.
   — Mary Oliver

If the world, without us, is what is beautiful —
If the rain coming on, regardless, is music —
If we are nothing in this world but what is in the way
        of a dance that hasn't and won't stop —
If we are only living here because there is nowhere else —
If the rain coming on is what is truly heroic, falling
        to lick the minor wounds of the earth —
Where will we go when we stop going on?

There are no answers, no awnings when I need them.
I have been thinking, all day, of Ben's voice, the push
and pull of blood in the body — not Ben's body,
my own. I imagine my cells stopping, one at a time.
If I get a cold, if I cut my hand and never heal —

Does heaven change? Does it change as the world does,
imitating Earth? The soul does — the individual boughs,
the waves, they break. And so do we, though our bodies don't
always, working and living on. Some animals can work their way

slowly out of the tired skin to be new again. My skin dies
so slowly before it finally goes, never wholly new.
I would like to think heaven knows change as we each do.
If we are not fixed, as we fear we are, in our days and our patterns,
then doesn't it learn with us? — the world is only what we bring
    to it.

4. Reprise

I am so afraid, and so afraid to say I am. Don't say you know,
of course you do. Who isn't afraid of something — maybe not
dying, but something. I'm afraid of dying like that.
And if I admit the chance, if the math works out and I could be

sick, then I have to be tested, which scares me as much
as the answer, because, in a way, it is an answer. Admitting
the danger is a danger in itself. I have life inside me
that isn't mine to lose. When I said to my mother

that I could die happy, she told me *No, don't,* as if my saying it
was enough to kill me. Outside, five children with yellow shirts
pulled over their clothes walk by, each holding another child's hand.
The cluster only has one speed. Careful

not to trip on the girl ahead of him, a boy lets go and is two feet
behind the group when the one adult cries out. I want to think
you are as afraid for me as I am. If you thought I wasn't safe,
you would call my name, wouldn't you? The boy catches up

and grabs her hand. I think you would. I'm happy I'm here
and so afraid to give you a reason to worry. I'm not yet ready to die.

That Moment, Remembering

Remembering when you first stopped believing in love
isn't as simple as it would seem. Your mother hasn't left
Christmas out, yet to be wrapped. Your father hasn't told you
that Mommy and Daddy don't love each other. It's more
than a moment, more like the realization of a moment.
Maybe your heart has been broken or you have broken
someone else's. You wake up alone again and again
or next to a lover who you don't love. For me, I just started
saying it — that love wasn't for me, that I didn't like the boys
at school, that they didn't like me. I told my mother
I didn't need anyone, and she cried, saying *Everyone
needs someone*. It wasn't long before I believed what I was
saying. It starts out small and gets too big for itself.
I was letting love exist for everyone but me, explaining
Valentine's Day. People who needed other people
named their need and named it Love. I told friends
they were enough for me. I pushed people away.

There is a moment you will remember believing in love again.
You may not remember believing, but you will remember
believing again. It's the moment you will remember
things your heart begged you to forget. For me, it was Ed.
He said he didn't need love, was happy on his own.
And he was wrong. It was the way he played with his straw
in the glass, how he didn't look me in the eyes —
and then didn't look away from them. I could tell
he didn't mean it, wondered if I sounded like that,
then wondered if I meant it. And the feeling rushed over me —
or rather, swept up from under the two of us.
He saw me grin and didn't ask why.

Portraits

1. Heat

I've been trying to write poems for him
because I'm finished or because I'm sorry.
I've been trying to write poems, long ones
that will make me remember or at least
understand. Nothing comes out
and all I can think of are the bottles left
without labels, broken or misplaced things.
I was told once that you can't remember pain,
like you can't remember heat. Maybe the bluest
flame or the smell of hair burning.
You can remember the sound a photo makes
as it curls in fire, but not the heat itself,
the very thing I want so badly to remember.

2. Photos

Not even a year after, I tried to describe him
to a friend who asked and all I could imagine
was a photograph of him that didn't quite capture
anything: his face buried into his sleeve, his hair
gelled and angular, not how I remember.
He looked like a child and I remembered a man.
So I wished I had kept more pictures. All along
I closed my eyes to bring him back, now nothing
came back to focus. I had lost him again.
But this time it made me so happy.

3. Turn

I thought if someone liked me, I must be okay. I thought
if someone was willing to hold me, I must be worth

not letting go. If someone liked my body, it was a good body.
If they liked my conversation, it was worthwhile. Why

do we give ourselves over to love, offer our hearts
as collateral for something we can't afford?

4. Morning Song

How does the morning do this, make you so beautiful?
How many poems have been written for lovers
in the morning light? I watch you sleep. Your arm

above the sheet, your fingers, the little hairs.
Is it this early light from the window, bright and not,
stretching into the room? This light does that.

The curve of ear and neck, the tangle and tuck
and lustrous hair — waking to something that hasn't
woken to you. I could love anyone in this gilding.

But I have loved you without it. For months,
you listened as I spoke of him, though you couldn't
stand to hear it. We stayed up late, talking.

I didn't know what you were thinking, only how
exhausted I was, only how untrusting. And because
it took so long to believe you, to give you that much,

there is already so much invested. I will hold you
until you wake up; I will let you have your dream
and let you be mine.

Shhh

You drive us home that night, stroke my leg like one
strokes an animal to calm him, though I am

so near sleep I feel guilty. You say *it's okay*
so I tilt my seat back, watch the lights

passing through the side mirror, stars slowly strung
like beads: quickly passing and aligning. Such

ease. Your hand rounds my knee and then back.
Slow pulse of the road, impossible to read

how fast we're going. *It's okay, go to sleep* but
I want to watch your reflection in the windshield. You are

the one who has to get up early. You are the one
who's been up all day and should be sleeping.

But you say *shhh* and I grip your hand,
unable to see the road and no need to.

Tattoo

for Ed

When you asked if I liked it did I say *No*,
because I can't understand such a strange desire

to advertise in print a picture that, today, you love?
Because the body is all we have? Because beauty

changes and cannot be worn forever? Did I say *No*,
tell you how I want to dissolve back into the earth

once I've died, have it take me back, not having revised
what I have been given? Did I push you away

because it seemed unnatural? I don't remember
what I said to you that morning as we spoke.

I knew it was a mistake, letting myself know
your skin — and later, how you wore the world,

or a favorite piece of it. I don't remember what I said, then,
but I'm glad you've shown me and glad you love

something enough to have it forever. I'm still learning to hold
something as long. To trust love, to really have it.

You gave yourself over to ink, knowing
what you wanted, and for how long.

Intimacy

Nico and I played this game — two months
without
fighting, I said *tell me something you
don't like*
and he paused as if to answer trivia, said
you don't
love me yet. And I said *I'm sorry.*
And then
it was my turn: *I don't know, everything
seems good,*
*we work surprisingly well. Anything that once
bugged me*
is now exactly what I want from you.
And then
(still my turn): *well, you don't share your
toothbrush.*
And he laughed, then said *I'm sorry too,
that's gross.*

The Promise

You have no reason to be afraid — you're fine.
You know that. But I have Ben on my shoulder
helping me count the white cells instead of sheep

as you sleep beside me. You expect this
to be so easy, asking me to recall each possibility
until I'm so scared and angry that you kiss my forehead

as if it's not safe. I am only a body to you,
a vessel of circumstance. And I want to cry
for how hard it is to admit I could be dying and how

easy it must be for you — but you begin to cry,
asking what we'll do if one of us is positive.
I don't want to think about it, turn away in the bed,

and am shocked to hear you say you'd want to stay.
Your family and friends will say *No*, but you will
tell them how I promised that I loved you.

Answer

We sit together in the lobby, reading magazines
from the previous year. I thought I would be so scared,
unable to wait for the results. I've let the blood
leave my body but want it back, afraid it contained

some secret, some unliving weight. But the time passed
and now we're in for the answer. The world
has paused, momentarily, to watch us walk up the steps,
sign in on the yellow sheet, take our seats.

I thought I'd panic in the still room. You went first
and I watched the television, telling the tragedies
bigger than me, bigger than both of us. We'll return
and they'll bring you back to life. It is only me now.

I thought of nothing, only watched the dim screen.
I didn't want this, I told you — meaning if it's positive
it isn't you that killed me, but if it is negative, it is you
I'll thank for bringing me back. I am finally called

and come back, saying nothing for a moment
before I smile.

Breakfast

for Nico

This is it, that comfortable crossing,
that uncrossing, going off, coming back.

This is it, that penny, found in a pocket.
I have a photograph of him

sleeping on a bench in a train station, waiting
to come home. I wish I had taken the picture,

but it was Veronica. They missed their train
and waited until six for another, while I waited

on tables in Gainesville. And when my cell phone shook
and I was with a table, I had to stop myself from answering

right then. Instead, I waited until my break to hear
the message: he yawned from over a thousand miles away

and when Veronica sang "untouchable face," I felt
as if I was right there, holding him.

          In the morning, I wake up early,
make him an omelet and bring him juice and we bend

around each other like crossed fingers. He hopes for a short day
and I hope for a long one beside him, but he goes to class

and I clean my room, or start to, read a little before putting it off.
I hope he finds that note in his pocket, the penny I snuck

into his shoe, and thinks of me, while I am here, thinking
of us. This is it, that tired, daily loving, that missing

or not missing. A thought as I put away the candles
and then wash the mess from breakfast. This is it, a picture of him

I found mixed with pictures of my family, that comfortable crossing,
uncrossing, going off, coming back. This is that moment

I know I can wait all day for him, all night, tomorrow.
That moment I'm not worried and glad I'm not. This is it.

Still Life

It isn't bright, exactly, but the water
has found what it can of the light.

The sky burns on the cold surface.
The mirror witnesses the bowing grass,
the trees left only with branches.

Everything is losing something
— even the water and sky are
giving their silver away. One by one,

the ibises and egrets claim bare branches
for the night. It is not simple how they come
to their places — gliding in,

they engage a hover, a hesitation
so deliberate it becomes a gesture in itself.
And then the wings fold — or rather unfold — under,

like the slack allowed by a puppeteer;
just the shoulders drop, and then the necks,
and then their whole bodies bend

as the branch shakes beneath them.
This is only motion. The true beauty
is in the assemblage, as one by one

the family comes into adagio.
But if the balance was lost — each pirouette
taken from its perch — could the scene survive

as still life? One bird is always preening
or applauding another — which is the essence,
the very glimmer of this waiting.

Each one returns, like love, to claim
or reclaim its share of the world.

Welcoming

When there is nowhere else to go, come here
to where you remember wanting

to leave, to where you used to know
nothing else. You're welcome here.

And in a way you welcome the place.
If you want love and don't remember

why, come here, watch yourself
settle in where you were once,

climbing onto the counter to spin
a prism your mother had left

hanging in the window. Watch yourself
lie on the linoleum, looking up

at the spinning room of color,
box of light, small space containing

so much. Watch yourself build
a little diorama of your history with love.

Look how still you lie and how long.
You don't want to leave

but you have to. There is nothing here
for you now. Remember first finding

the cabinet your father used
to hold the artifacts of your life:

yellowing painting, report cards, letters
to Santa. Remember him

finding you there, crying. Not knowing
how to tell him why. It's okay to come here.

Everyone else has left; the house is quiet.

Moth

I know neither how to open nor to close.
    —Peter Sirr

How does it happen? That flicker in the dark
like a candle lit and then blown out.
The smoke after, the smell of it. I need you

to hear this. Do you ever stop, halfway?
Or having crossed the street, do you ever cross back
to look more closely at something in the road?

Do you walk on? Washing dishes,
do you catch yourself wandering
toward the light on the glass?

I don't know, finally, how to love.
And yet I do. Daily and wholly,
and not only people. We live:

stop at the bank, have a cup of coffee,
forget to write, remember to lock the door.
How often do we live,

having that steady nostalgia even as we live it,
feeling memory create itself as we stand there,
wandering? Wondering? Both, I think, together.

Do you ever wonder if these moments
are what life really is? These lit moments
you rise into will be what is cut together

to finally be your life. We open into it,
we catch ourselves, and we stop. Who saw me
staring into the candle like that?

What must they imagine I'm thinking?
Let us catch ourselves opening
and then catch ourselves stopping

and not. Let us open and open,
without knowing how.